T0317323

LOGOTHERAPY

African POETRY
BOOK SERIES

Series editor: Kwame Dawes

LOGOTHERAPY

Mukoma Wa Ngugi

University of Nebraska Press / Lincoln and London

"Hunting Words with my Father" appeared in
Mythium Journal 3 (Summer 2011); "I Swear
I See Skulls Coming" appeared in *New York
Quarterly* 65 (Winter 2009); "A Poem for Arthur
Nortje" appeared in *Kwani Journal* 2 (2003).

The African Poetry Series has been made possible
through the generosity of philanthropists
Laura and Robert F. X. Sillerman, whose
contributions have facilitated the establishment
and operation of the African Poetry Book Fund.

Library of Congress
Cataloging-in-Publication Data
Names: Mũkoma wa Ngũgĩ, author.
Title: Logotherapy / Mukoma Wa Ngugi.
Description: Lincoln: University
of Nebraska Press, [2016]
Series: African book poetry series
Identifiers:
LCCN 2016003755 (print)
LCCN 2016010483 (ebook)
ISBN 9780803290679 (pbk.: alk. paper)
ISBN 9780803295308 (epub)
ISBN 9780803295315 (mobi)
ISBN 9780803295322 (pdf)
Classification:
LCC PR9381.9.M778 A6 2016 (print)
LCC PR9381.9.M778 (ebook)
DDC 821/.92—dc23
LC record available at
http://lccn.loc.gov/2016003755

Set in Garamond Premier by Rachel Gould.
Designed by N. Putens.

For my wife, Maureen Burke, and daughter, Nyambura Eileen Wa Mukoma. Without you my words have no music.

CONTENTS

ACKNOWLEDGMENTS

With gratitude and debt to Kwame Dawes and Matthew Shenoda for their warm but deep critical reading and for giving these poems a home. Much warmth to the IPPP writers and musicians (what the hell does our acronym stand for again?) Melissa Tuckey, Krishna Ramanujan, and Joe Crookston. And to Joeth Zucco for letting me see, enter, and be swallowed up by the poems once again. I am also thinking of Clifton Gachagua—that poetic volcano that is the future!

LOGOTHERAPY

I

To Give a Word a Name

Preface

(For my father's seventieth)

One morning I burst into my father's study and said
when I grow up, I too want to hunt, I want to hunt
words, and giraffes, pictures, buffalos, and books

and he, holding a pen and a cup of tea, said, *Little Father,
to hunt words can be dangerous—but still, it is best to start
early.* He waved his blue *bic-pen* and his office turned

into Nyandarua forest. It was morning, the mist rising
from the earth like breath as rays from the sun fell hard
on the ground like sharp nails. *Little Father, do you see*

him?—my father asked. No, I said. *Look again—the mist
is a mirror—do you see him?* And I looked again and
there was a Maasai warrior tall as the trees, spear in hand.

*Shadow him, feign his movements, shadow him until
his movements are your movements.* Running my feet
along the leaves I walked to where he was, crouched

like him so close to the earth, feet sinking deeper
into the earth as if in mud, turning and reading the wind
and fading into the mist till I became one with the forest.

For half a day we stayed like this—tired and hungry
I was ready for home. But my father said, *I did not say
this was easy—you cannot hunt words on a full stomach.*

And just as soon as he spoke there was a roar so loud
and stomping so harsh that hot underground streams broke
open like a dozen or so water pipes sending hissing,

steaming water high into the air. I turned to run
but the warrior stood his ground. As the roar
and thunder came closer, his hair braided and full of red

ochre turned into dreadlocks so long that they seemed like
roots running from the earth. When the transfiguration
was complete, before me stood a Mau Mau fighter, spear

in one hand, homemade gun in the other, eyes so red
that through the mist they looked like hot molten
cinders, the long dreadlocks a thousand thin

snakes in the wind, the leaves and grass and thorns
rushing past him. *You must help him, don't just stand
there, help him*—my father implored but just as soon

as I had closed my little hands into fists, the lion
appeared high up in the air, body stretched the whole
length as the Mau Mau fighter pulled the spear like

it was a long root from the earth. The lion, midair, tried
to stop, recoiled its talons to offer peace, but it was too
late and it let out another roar as its chest crushed

into the spear, breastplate giving way until the spear
had edged its way to the heart. Dying then dead
it continued its terrible arc and landed. I waved

and the picture stood still. My father came up to me
and asked, *Why have you stopped the hunt?* I said

"but we killed it—I have what we came for." I pointed

to where the Mau Mau warrior was pulling his spear
from the carcass, but my father shook his head and said
—*You have done well but look closely—how can you*

carry all that in a word? How can we carry that home?
It is too heavy. I laughed and said—"Father, you help me."
But he pointed to the ground, to a steady flow of a bright

thin red river furiously winding down from the grooves
of the spear to the earth. I too pointed, unable to speak
—the beauty larger than my imagination. I was confused.

I had no words. *Come, let us go home Little Father.*
When you are of age you shall find the words, he said.
But always be careful—to hunt a word is to hunt a life.

Ancestries of Land Mines

I

As children we walk without hungering for old age—perfect
little gods made out of clay. Names and things bear your name
but if life is not willed, death will find you. Make clay that
hardens to hold a memory—a thing that cannot trace steps
walked is dead even as it draws breath.

II

Gifts. Rain. To see the world anew. Breathe wet air
cigarette in hand, sneakers in sewer ground, jeans dragging
the day's germs home. In the dark you keep stepping
into your shadow blackened to your skin by night. As a child
in the dark, you could not mirror yourself.

III

Walking home, remnants of yourself drip from remembrances
black ink erodes your skin into the wet road, black islands
for tour guides, blind canes pointing to where you fade and die
each time you are born. Each time you die they say
they loved their neighbor. How they loved your shadows!

IV

As a child, freedom is named after the stomach of needs
even those that we imagine. One day, when the vote first burns
in your imagination, before Soweto Passes ignite like paper tigers
you will feel solidarity because you dreamt it first
and find license to steal the happiness that once rode trains.

V

A train—multiplicity of symbols, departure, arrival,

whirling between worlds and destinations. Beware
of all movement. To resemble the earth is to be without
a constant face. Stand and you will revolve
to be one amongst others like you.

VI

Love is not to be sanitized in its furiousness, beauty
is in the gutters. It travels the spectrum between
hell and the rainbow—where the God sleeps after
we birthed it. Slay it once, then again. Then find love
sufficient to hold the earth's wound close to your open chest.

VII

As a child now half adult, moons and suns wore different faces.
When you learned to say Africa, it wore the face of your home's
wooden planks that cried in the rain, and dried still expressions
that doves could not sing into a song. Refugee child walking along
intricate boundaries to find home in starved margins.

VIII

Landscapes of so many faces, truths of landscapes, the blues
the sukus, salsa, jazz, Lingala, the rumba—and the Tizita
all rhythms to the same step—the swish of chains against the ocean
winds. A word alone skates to sing, we remain at sea waiting to sink
an oar into the next blue wave.

IX

The world evolves in small infinite steps. Where we don't grow
mugumo trees in our backyards, the mirror of another grows and feeds
our children strange fruits. Refugee child learns to hold a gun
walking along boundaries without spilling into land mines of ancestry
—Nkurumah's natural-born child soldier of no borders.

X

A newborn child like a fruit falls to her parents' feet. If they don't walk
then she must learn from her grandparents. If they too stood still
if their world was always still like a photograph, then it must trust
its infant footsteps to draw a map of Africa as one molds clay.
And unlike our god, she must learn to die for her creation.

Keys

(For Nyambura)

By the time she was two, my three-year-old daughter
had her own set of play keys, keys that her mother,
and her aunt Robin played with as children. I imagine
that for her, these little jingling things that we cannot
leave home or without which we cannot every now
and then open our fire safety box to add one more
diploma or contract are powerful if not magical totems.
But somewhere around the age of nine or ten or whenever children
earn the right to close and open the doors to their lives, keys
will be yet another thing not to leave the house without
like her lunch box, homework, or a cellphone by its other name
then. And some day, when her mother and I are long gone,
or, more cheerfully, old and with secrets pouring out
of our demented minds faster than the life oozing out
of us, and our grandchildren are playing with keys that once
opened the doors to our lives and secrets, will she realize
as I do now that all that remains of all those things locked
in our safes is a random set of play keys, unattached?

My Two Names

I have tried but am never hungry in Nairobi and full in Boston.
No matter my will the parallels will not collapse—it is a synchronized
stomach this one. Sometimes I try for daylight here to surprise
nightfall there. But right in the divide of night and day
the sun is lodged in such a place that I am always awake here
and asleep there.

I am without a name. Yet, I bear two names.
I am without a name. I bear four names. I am nameless.

II

Always outside my window, my shadow restless likes a ghost
calls me to find its parallel. When I left home, I found
it here dancing with rope, an effigy outlined in chalk and we took
turns as shadow and being.

When I close my eyes to this sun or moon born still, the world around
me keeps changing form and I make a home. But flight
too has a shadow, and I fall back into things I cannot name
or touch. What I cannot name I cannot touch.

One day I will have to speak to myself.

III

One day, in my bones, marrow deep and complete like a grenade,
I find remnants of those that walked and lived hard before me
Arthur Nortje-Can Themba, Marechera—all born in times when
to imagine collapse of parallels was as treacherous as treason.

IV

Home is longing not to be in two places at once.
This morning there I woke up to sounds of mourning and tear gas,
graves as shallow as my writing paper
deep like diamonds and coal mines.

This morning here I awoke to a cup of tea with fresh ginger and mud
—someone's black blood. There, this morning thirty years
ago, I witness Kimathi's hanging. This morning here
thirty Puerto Rican nationalists were hanged.

One day I will have to speak to all of ourselves.

To Our Unborn Child Whom
We Shall Name Nyambura

It is 7:49 p.m.—your mother, and you—twelve weeks now—are making black beans garnished with corn—I think—at the point you are reading this you will see what I mean—sometimes what she cooks is undecipherable, like the old texts from Timbuktu. You have both been eating a lot. This exhausted chef is in his office writing.

For the purposes of present writing, I mean writing in real time and speaking to you, I shall now taste what she has made—before that let me mention she also brought me a fork—expected—and a napkin—unexpected—she got a haircut today—but that is neither here nor there.

About that bite. After letting the steam escape, which carried with it the fragrance of garlic and onion, I then took a bite—it was good, this heap—do not be misled by the word *heap*—whatever it was, it was tasty.

When you get to know me you will wish I had kept more of these notes, and then you will get to know me well enough and you will know I only wrote to you, let's face it, when I had to. This, on my first day of writing to you, I want you to know—you will enter this world loved—by your mother and I—You were loved even before you were born.

Well—that is the pleasant stuff. But this I want you to know also—you have made your mother change—her hips expanding, her breasts sore, she has had to postpone her boards (if you become a writer that will mean a dart board and if you become a doctor, that will be mean—well, what it means). Also unpredictable foods and tastes—now you have made her hate my oxtail soup but love those sundaes topped with gluten-free brownies—your taste I must presume.

We worry, and we love. The world you will be born in—what responsibility shall we take for it? The questions you will have and demand of us—what answers shall we have? I hit a deer on my way to see your mother over Thanksgiving—I was calm—and she was calm—I cannot imagine a world, no, it would be an unjust world, a wrong world if I was not there to greet you. In this, my first note to you—know that even though we joke, a little alien has taken over your mother's body, you were born into love.

Oops, have to go now—a friend is calling me from Edison's, my beer is almost done anyway—and your mother is going to bed.

In Your Name

(For Nyambura)

Bringer of Rain, I know someday I will learn
to call you by the name your mother and I gave you.
But for now the myriad of little names
will do—gacucu, kamii, Karii, Nyam2
N2—all names that amuse us now
as often as they will not you.

Kamii—ka-shitter, or Karii, ka-eater, you will abandon
let's face it, even hate me for having them in a poem.

But Kamami—little mother—you will not abandon. Yes, it will first tie
you down, tongue-tie your teachers and friends, but one day
your name, Nyambura, will free you, and that which
was once like a prison will be a warm embrace and that past
from which you come will be an anchor and not a chain.
Each syllable, a reminder, an echo.

A Moment between Writing

(For Nyambura)

At fifteen months old—here comes your will. Naptime—I rush to my computer. Mid-sentence you wake up. You decide that you should be dressed only after you have your shoes on. The world does not work that way, I say. Is this a battle worth fighting? Food for peace, I go to the kitchen. You crawl up the stairs up to your room, bring down one shoe, you continue crying. The stairs again, the other shoe. I would like to believe that moment changed you because you realized you could make the world move—I don't know—all I can tell you is that after that moment you changed and you became a small devil of your own will. And we loved you for it!

An Orange

You might think that unlike bananas
so useful in baking bread, making splits,
and in showing the absolutely 100%
correct way of wearing a condom
that oranges are limited to making fresh juice
with or without pulp. But think back to when
as a child an orange was a picture with a name
to be learned alongside apples and giraffes
or became the sun on those days when the mist
was so thick that it reflected your face back when
you pressed it against the window or became a soccer
ball when bouncing objects like tennis balls
were banned from the living room. Yes an orange
might not have the coolness of a banana, but I dare
you a banana peel in that perfect martini, or if you
are like me, old but still rough on the edges, a slice
of banana to complete a whiskey-filled old-fashioned.

Pepto Bismol

Napoleon, no mustache but twice a halved Hitler
found it decreed by the oracle cow dung, and a witch
doctor that he be in envy of the black nose.
A sling slang not unlike David's, he rode to Egypt

in search of Pharaoh, thinking a black face had
a softer forehead than Goliath. On finding African
slaves emptied into the Americas, "Forward troops"
our halved hero yelled, but alas, the salty swim bloated

one too many a stomach, and ill winds blew due to too
much broken wind. The battlefield—swords thrust—
his ballooned stomach. That is how Pepto Bismol
came about and Waterloo got its name!

Multiplicity and Skins

I

In Boston's summer heat, my skin is stretched taut like a tent,
sweat drops roll off, impervious to skin like rain on iron sheets.
Under this my shelter, veins squeeze violent blood through
capillaries. The calm mummer of an erupting volcano—how
much feeling the universe must have had a second before
explosion of singularity—I walk slowly, my skin a map
of what it was, might have become, could become—the snap
of my umbilical cord has unbalanced my step, somewhat
unhinged my world—even madness invents its own logic.
Here you have to imagine the surprise of a snake shedding
its first skin till losing of skin becomes instinct of renewal,
but then again there is the agony of the moth that transmutes
into silk but come winter stands naked—I carry my shed skins
in my briefcase, a photo album of things I have been.

II

At another time, I wanted to say that the dying do not care
for dying and the living for the living, the perfect paradox
but that was when prophecy came to me easy like death.
Strained, I wipe my face with my palm for sweat
and fever and my face imprints on my hand, wipe
again and it falls onto my palm. I walk home a naked
skull with its face in hand. At a red traffic light,
pedestrian that I am, I pause to study it, wondering
how long before another grows in place. This one,
I loved the best, could have been me, this is the face,
skin I could have become. Folding it into my briefcase
I step into the street. Home, journal in hand, I erase myself
onto a page but I find biography knows nothing of itself,
certainly not the inside of a word. When they asked me
what I was doing when the revolution came, I said
I was at home waiting for my face to grow.

Safe House

Sirens trespass through our bar window
and a mess of red lights dance disco
on our writing pads.

We will not follow the dead
or the dying, the child to be saved
or born still, the old man whose engine

has died mid-stroke, or the victim
of multiple gunshots. We will not
follow those dying from just living.

The ambulance passes by and we
remain snouts dipped in a river's
rush only lifting up our heads

to let the roar pass. Neither
predator nor prey, and at times one
or the other, we are poets in a safe

-house made out of spit and words.
We continue drinking one life
as another, others pass us by.

Shadows and Light

Shadows and Light in Play

What starts on all four then stands on two and ends on three?
—A Human Being
—African riddle

PREFACE

I wring my folding brain for a word. It says,
it is not good to keep your lungs folded—

scream!—but scream the snap of a guitar string.
It tires. It stops. It's abrupt. Classical suicide

on stage. From where I sit wearing silhouettes
of lights and shadows, I can peer into the guitarist's

soul lighted center stage. It screams—dispense
with the guitar and dance—I cannot be contained

by the neck of your guitar—another string—
the band plays on—and another string snaps. I fold

my pen into my shirt pocket—I learn. I exit.
I will not cheat my pen to speak of form

(Stage Directions: Going out—preacher at Roxbury Bus Station)

At Roxbury Bus Station, work, yawns, hate,
love left home, grief—it is the human
market for tethered emotions—to this stream,
or plethora if you like—a preacher bathed green

by the glow of his new BMW—to this human stream,
he preaches with a megaphone—may his word *not* find
fertile ground—how useful a *haiku* would be for him
of a thousand words. The bus is here, everyone must
have a destination—we climb in—soon I shall
be at Wally's Jazz Bar

(Photograph of a woman by a jukebox at Wally's Jazz Bar)

In light that fades into shadow, a black hand,
confidence conferred by still of camera emerges
to face perplexity of selection. It is a song neither
she or I will hear. Her hand always folds back into
her shadow or does it always bring back light? Modern-day
John Keats, sometimes, I wonder after the surprise
of the Urn's children when they learn in English 101
that their parents never fucked. The fact of their birth.
The fact of the urn. The fact of the literary critic.
I am getting bored by my thoughts.

(Dream sequence after too much beer)

Walking. Under my feet rocks and underground streams
that I follow to a surprise of a hot springs and geyser.
I sit by its basin. Dreams erase exile. I am almost home.
A voice says, "Leaving you that evening was not easy."
I sit and I think "these rocks are older than I am yet I am not small.
The world is older than me. I live in its belly, yet at some point
it will be younger than me—I will be the center. I will stand
in the middle of time—one second later the center
will shift—let us live then for we each die our own death."
I follow the underground stream back. In the desert, grass grows
along its banks and animals eat—"we must not stray far
from our source," the Voice says.

From the hot spring, I am inhaling sulfur,
my eyes mist and through their glass I look
inward. I am about to see the past—my lungs
constrict, I am drowning and I have no gills,
the beauty of fish, a twelve-second memory
and as such their world always begins anew.
Imagine this, being birthed into light
and ocean green seaweeds at such
a frequency. Embrace the world anew!
Love it anew! Discover it anew! Life
is to be without memory, death is the murder
of memory. I open my brain in search of time,
I see her again—smile frozen in welled
dimples—the beauty—to own it I must
not awaken. I try to peer past today
but I keep ending where I slept, my footsteps
end at the bank of yesterday, I wish to be awake,
I try and fail, I will again and I wake up to the sun.

(Waking up)

I wake up in the streets. The sun is a thousand daggers
tearing into my eyes, my lips dry and sanded by the sun break
into blood, my book bag full of yesterday's manuscripts,
this faithful dog lies at my feet—fingerprints
of a careless drunk hand. The guitar string
keeps snapping in my head, mute abrupt thuds that find
rhythm in the beat of my heart. I have invited hell
into the streets. I walk past the debris, there was a riot
here last week—the president has refused to die.

(Sequences of walking home)

I

Walking past Dana-Faber hospital, a doctor
without scalpel and makeup streaked
like a dirty rainbow wails. Even on my unsure
feet, I stand and watch. Too early to call relatives
full of hope, let them sleep, they have a lifetime
to grieve. I think—*bless you dear doctor for letting them*
rest before their grief realizes its infinite
possibilities—children, spouses, relatives, friends,
co-workers, etc.—each death touches all, sends
echoes to every life, we all inherit each death—I walk
on—let the dead bury their dead and living bury the living

(Thoughts on observations as I get on Blue Hill Avenue)
Even in this ungodly hour, the choir by the church on my street
practices to sing to a dead God and Ogun—our deity of iron, trapped
between life and death, being born and dead—cannot find his way
home—he cannot forge spear or assegai, his is the space between
hammer and anvil. The chorus, a mummer of many rivers spills
into the street, screams above traffic, it rises above and around the
earth—it ascends until it dissipates. But in this interlude that spells
summer's heat of hell, I cannot help but wear their voices. Let the
choir drive my voices into the sea—I sit by the church's stairway, cup
my head on a tripod of arms to stare into tomorrow. What do I see?
What is there to see? Prophet of yourself what shall you sing?

(Almost home, at the intersection)

At the cornerstone where Woodville Street intersects
Blue Hill Avenue, at the pay phone a woman
cuts link, umbilical cord to love. The slap
of the handset coming down cuts into my folding
brain. The guitar string snaps. Right at the moment

of hanging up and her taking steps of liberation
onto the street, the red light turns green and spills
traffic. Tires try to hold onto tarmac. I think how often
it is that death loves only those who are free

(At home I find a play in a play)
*(Stage Directions: Late morning, the sun keeps ascending from its hell
echoes of yesterday. She sits at the kitchen table, cup of coffee in hand,
hands a tripod. The kitchen is small with a stove and two chairs. He
walks in, sits down, and lights a cigarette. He looks up as the smoke
ascends into the whirling fan to find death. It is otherwise quiet.)*

Where have you been?
Walking back.
To where?
Just walking back, backward—to the beginning—looking for time.
Did you find anything?
No, not very much.
No?
Just that life and death are the same footstep.
What does that mean?
I don't know—I need to sleep—I am asleep—I have been asleep

*(He walks to another room. She picks up a paintbrush, dips it in red ink,
and continues with a painting—it is important that the audience does
not see it—lights fade.)*

(Interlude of a thought in my head as the play opens)

I have no use for the past—still—to you, I have walked
backward followed underground streams,
last night's bread crumbs to the beginning,
yet each morning, regardless of what I dream,
I must start again where I slept—and even

when I peer into tomorrow, I cannot see
you past yesterday—let memory bury
remembrance—I can see why you must leave,
but do you also see why I must also leave
if only to return?

(Loss begins bearing down as I leave home to sit by the lake)

II

Buoyed by the righteous departure—the pain of losing
limb for freedom, I am a martyr of loss. By the lake, the water
and ice move lazily like folding, mangled glass—winter will
simply not let up. I dip my left foot in. Like hungry fish, shards
of broken ice crowd around my ankle. I have been anointed,
yet even in these shards I cannot see even half my face.

III

I limp back to the pier. I stare deep into the water.
I jump in. The frozen glass gives in. I am not worried,
I cannot die in my own womb but into what shall
I birth myself? I am without hands, fuck the senses,
I am without them all. Where shall I bury my placenta?
I do not remember. Must I begin once again?

IV

The paradox of erasure is this—we never begin
where we ended—the paradox of being is this—
memory is a foothold for both life and death.
Happiness was intoxication—your hands, tendrils
that found root where I began—yet without your eyes
here to light yesterday, your black-and-white
photograph says—I am a riddle—I am the ghost
of a happy past—remember me a thousand times
for a thousand tears—what am I? I wear my skin

to remind me of sorrow, these tortured scales, let me
wade in it for a little while.

v

But even when I chose to forget—the sun always rises—it has said
it will rise—the crust of the earth dries, lava rises—the spread
of a splintering eggshell, it mummers, it crackles, the clay crusts
into dry rivulets—then the rebirth and I am born anew, skin a wound
that will be shed before I learn to walk again—Lazarus resurrected
—there is no one true death my wailing friend—see, here I am with
the walk of an infant. Young voices are old and aged voices
learn to sing—hear the ululations, the trumpet triumphs
where the god of iron died—I cannot be blinded twice
without learning to see.

EPILOGUE

A volcano, a pendulum frozen in mid-stroke,
on its own will, it thaws. It erupts and strikes the clock
midnight. The abundant lava, it is what I must
use to mend missing limbs and skin left in the snares
of a thousand hunters. Onto these bones
which acid has eroded to their whiteness, I distill
hot lava onto them, I flesh the scarecrow. I take
a first step onto a busy street, the sun is uneven
on my skin. Look! Look! The children scream—a scarecrow
with human flesh. You must not be scared that I am
a little bent out of shape and my scars all uneven—
we are patches of many things, you must understand.
You must not be contained by the form of the earth.
The ugliest face is that unscarred by rebellion.

The Clouds Above

Hunting for wet clay in the marshlands

of Limuru, my sister and I would spot

a plane, pause, clap, laugh, and yell AMERICA

to stamp our hopes on the passing dream.

But for children in Pakistan and Somalia

the open sky is no longer the place to send

dreams to catch a flight abroad. The skies

camouflage predator drones that track

and hunt their dreams. Imagine that.

A sky that is no longer a promise. And clouds

that can bring down rain—or death.

A Walk amongst Shadows with Sandra

In Boston, Charles River runs through this city of big digs
old buildings and new stairways to new gods at the Fenway
it runs by universities and disco clubs and cuts into two clean
halves, a lover's park. But in having a little bit of everything,
a little bit of everything is lost and as such there is no perfect
solitude. Yet we must find it so Sandra and I keep walking
along pathways that bend with the river and groan under
the weight of runners, cyclists, and lovers trailing behind
small portable dogs. Around and behind us our
shadows keep changing form—long, small, oblong, starved.

Soon, the sun gives ground to the street lamps snaking
alongside the river. Under the sparse thin trees we keep
losing our shadows only to find them strangely pale and ill
under the yellow streetlights, before breaking into many
shadows stretched thin between the lights. We have
multiplied yet we are afraid of touch and I keep thinking
about the day when I first saw you walking along
Charles River as though through a black-and-white still
photograph, coloring love on all that remained in the wake
of your traveling shadow.

Perfect Silence Is When Each Thing Sings Itself

Standing outside

with the rain

gone

droplets roll

down rooftop

gutters

straining drop

by drop

till a rough wind

making its way home

through the Acacia trees

turns trickles

of water

to surprise waterfalls.

Perfect silence is never silent.

Perfect silence is when each thing sings itself.

Geysers and Hot Springs

Winter is still. Incisive wind.
Spring grows hesitant
the sun still tender
but promise enough
and laughter once frozen
begins to thaw
and its small trickles
reach the street outside the Puerto Rican Bar
where I pause in step and walk in.

Inside, I am twice a tourist
muted by language and skin
but the blood
that runs through the salsa
beats in me, I swear I would recognize
it anywhere.

In the streets of Nairobi, foreignness
is to be occupied. Here we see each other
in the coarse loving hands of absences.

Stepping outside, winter
and night have shelled the sun
back into the sky,
but the merengue
lights my way home.

Bifocals

Now that I am almost there I can tell you—
your eyes are the first to go. And with that
comes the stories that begin with the lie,
my, you haven't changed a bit since kindergarten.

My eyesight was so good I could make out a fly
buzzing above the I-90 West signposts as I drove
across little towns at the speed of light.

My eyesight was so good that I got an award
for the most 20/20 sighted motherfucker
to ever set foot in a New York DMV.

My eyesight was so good . . .

But sooner or later the warning—
OBJECTS ARE CLOSER THAN THEY APPEAR,
newspaper print,
a cookbook,
simple instructions to building an IKEA desk
a PowerPoint presentation.
Sooner or later, the indignity of pulling out
a pair of bifocals from their oiled leather pouch,
and the unpracticed awkward wearing that at first

lances you ears (and at least once up your nostril),
and the feeling that you cannot shake of someone,
an older sibling perhaps, holding a finger
an inch from your face and saying "but I am not even
touching you" and your turn to tell the inevitable joke,

"My eyesight was so good that I found needles in haystacks
for play."

I say, you once could see but now you can bling.
Go on, with the prostate about to go,
go on and wear them bifocals.

New Frontiers

Standing by Lake Mendota, even with a brave
sun bouncing off heavy snow rocks, my winter
jacket is wrapped tight like a second skin, my naked

face the frontier of the battle between heaven and hell.
Soon my lips will split in a thousand places, the wind
chill negative an inhumane number like minus twenty-six

torture of a thousand pins. The natives
keep saying this has been a warm winter, much warmer
than last year. They say, *in 1902* [sometimes I find it's 2001

1807 or some random year] *ten children, fifteen old men,*
two Africans, and a herd of Jersey cows died. This is nothing.
I light a cigarette for wood. Spring will be here soon to forget

this winter and its dead. Yes, for each one of us there are two
deaths—your natural death, the life you die in your flesh
and always to be remembered less than what you really were.

I. Excerpts from an Immigrant's Diary

Unroll film. Damn it I have to borrow my neighbor's
TV. "It's more reasonable to borrow a VCR,
an iron, or a screwdriver, but not the damn TV.
Why not a hammer instead, or salt?" she asks when I point
at her nice coffee table and porcelain dishes to set.
"Why don't you take a photograph of my apartment?"
she offers. "Won't be my apartment now, will it?" I say
gently. So I had to prop her TV on two pairs of old
cowboy boots stuffed with stones. Photographs,
I am pleased to say, capture a certain degree
of affluence and my artistic nuances. Last time they sent
me money, I took it to the bar across the street
and bought many happy liquid poems.

II. FROM LETTER FED-EXED IN THE MORNING

Do you carry me with you? I walked back to the
night we first met, when we learned to run
in a sack holding potatoes on spoons. How
we used to walk down anonymous stairs
as if it was down the aisle. I put up
your photograph every now and then when
it's not infinitely easier to find a nearer
you. Happy belated Birthday!!
PS/ Without me, can you possibly be happy?

III. FROM THE REPLY

There is nothing here, not even mad people
except the lady next door who walks her little bitch
every morning to remind me of you!

Whispers and Tendrils

First Meetings

(For Maureen)

I have no name, just you, backpack hunched
over your shoulders like a turtle's nest, and thin
dark spectacles to protect the sapphire (I learn

later) in your eyes. It is midday. Over
lunch, with my friends we are boys again
full of conspiracies and girls. My food cold

I run them through this first image and I think
how your short black hair does not take
to the wind. Are we to remain without names?

First Date

(For Maureen)

In courtship even anecdotes are epic
and we stop to converse and count
passing cars, walk again until East
Lansing, this pebble of a city is behind
us and past love affairs are spent
and siblings, relatives, and friends
are all accounted for and white
and black skins left for nearby Klansmen
and dreams of doctors and writers
are in front of us. We find a stream
and a bench and sit to watch a few
renegade ducks leave webbed trails
that shimmer in the moonlight.
You and I, we have only spoken
ourselves until that first kiss
that drills wells so deep
the stream becomes a river.

Framing Your Picture

(For Maureen)

Takes a long time to find the right frame,
and longer still to decide on framing you.
Thrift store to thrift store. No! This one
will not do, looks too much like a prison.
That one reeks of ownership. This one
—a bad poem—it hides nothing.
And . . . who wants to be seen through glass
like a mannequin? But this love of ours
has friends, and Paul brings an old frame.
It stands on iron. It will not bend or break.
Not a prison but a fortress. It will do.
Over the phone I ask—have you by any chance
been feeling protected? You laugh.
I shall leave you framed.

Framing a Second Picture

Strange habits because here I am again
sifting through St. Vincent's shelves.
If I was any older they would start calling
me a crazy old man with a thing for thrift
stores and picture frames, but youth shields
me until I find the perfect frame—an open air
frame. Here you can spill outside to find
sun and dust, salsa or Lingala. The aroma
of my ginger salmon . . . Over the phone
that evening, it is your photo that gives
me comfort and I realize you—my modern-
day witch—can be at two places at the same time.

Guttural Love

(For Maureen)

Until this morning, I hadn't realized it
—that between the space of sleep

and awakening, fatigued by travel
in our dreams and becoming known

we have taken to guttural
love. Here I grunt you a glass

of water—there you grunt me your
hand—here I grunt you the silenced

alarm, there slipping out of bed you grunt.
I grunt you a cup of tea—and our day

begins. What language —sound
is this we have given love?

Love and Distance

(For Maureen)

In East Lansing, by this stream that once washed a steel
worker clean—we trace love by a cobbled foot

path—it moves so uncertain of itself—your hand
in my hand—first meetings. Back in Madison

just so I can be closer to you, I walk for miles
by lake Mendota—dirtiest water I have ever

seen—beer cans and dead fish staring back
algae choking form—and I think—regardless

I like walking here just to dream of water, when
you are away I walk love to think of loving you.

Leper's Gold

Outside, at home, through open
blinds I stare into a stranger's
house, their rituals before bed
one glass of wine by a bed stand
and I wonder what you see
when you look through my window.

Nostalgia I

I

How far back will I walk
to find you as I remember?

II

It's with you that our shadows had feelings,
touching even when our bodies stood apart.

III

At the lake, this oasis in a small coal mine city
a wooden bench, a bottle of wine and old letters

IV

Looking back, the lake could be here, in Cleveland
even Boston.

V

This photograph, or a painting hanging on a wall,
this song, these colors—all you? I cannot
regret you, or loving you.

VI

Etcetera.

Nostalgia II

I

The night is without sight. The distant
river purrs and reflects light enough to die
at its banks, and where it has dug deep,
it is a valley thin like the string of a blind moon
rising out of the earth. No fishermen cast their
nets here and even the grass has retreated
from the thinning banks to safety where we sit
dew soaked. To touch either vow or promise,
I stretch my damp hand only to feel the heat
rising out of where she molded her figure out
of the earth's clay—I did not hear her leave—
she would not let me hear her leave. Above
the purr of the river, a train with windows
lit like dull stars is pulling away.

II

A word planted in her beauty slows down
and softens my earth, it implodes then scatters
a thousand fireflies that light even the hardest
of nights, a relay race in a summer Olympic
galaxies that ease the sun into daylight.
But when even a nightmare is a warm blanket,
waking up is always a violent affair. I light
a cigarette, inhale deeply, and exhale to watch
smoke rings, filtered through the sun's rays
ascend to the ceiling fan then dissipate to die
in my place. At night, before sleep, I can still
dream this ascension—only now it wears two
wedding rings. Does it matter then
"whether I wake or sleep?"

A Poem Written in Silence

(For Oulanje Regan)

Freezing that glint of a tear in my memory, scared of my own,
I sought refuge in my four-door cage—leaving was inevitable
as our meeting again I hoped. I was grateful (your quiet
neighborhood did not think so as I saw them looking through
drawn blinds) that my muffler was in three distinct pieces.
I immersed myself in the blaring sound of moving engine,
surrendering feeling to sound. (I imagined I was a race car
driver.) I did take a peek through my rearview mirror before
I turned off Silvan Road onto Oak Hearst Avenue, and I
saw you waving. I wanted to turn back, but the gods were not quick
to honor the schizophrenia that accompanies flight—and from
33 East to 2nd Street I kept ringing your doorbell over and over again—
"Break down" I ordered my old but faithful blue Plymouth to stem
the growing distance but to no avail. (It did however fall apart four days
after arrival.) Did I sound disappointed when I called to say
I had just arrived?

Last Frames

(For Sandra)

I

Behind every revelation, there remains just as much
without prophecy. It is here that our evening began
pleasantly enough, light conversations on days schemed,
little things like the secrets in your shopping
bag, how the pub with church stained windows
reminds you of Dublin, and then how you
must leave me before you leave. Should I have knelt
or remained standing?

II

A strand of your hair in mine, little notes, birthday cards
songs, touch, dreams.

III

If indeed words did use you and me so that they may be spoken
then let the whole damn world come undone in order to be said.

IV

Remembrances

A Poem for Arthur Nortje and
Other Lost African Poets

Your forehead jutting outward swelling with the wretchedness
of inheritance, watching your trail of black dust, ashes
of a cremated past swirl and twirl, a dance with voiceless ghosts
that see through the film of your eyes. Your eyes frozen deep
in the monotony of the past holding a black-and-white
photograph of a stillborn baby's wail. Your nails thrust

deep into the palm of your right hand until it explodes
like a grenade reading blood will flood the River Nile,
your reflection lies facedown in the Thames River, I see
a corpse in an ocean-sized fitting room. Consult neither
the Yoruba gods nor oracles, what you need is an internal shift
of perception, find beauty sufficient enough to thaw feeling.

Once you found beauty and said a true word, one true word spills
its truth at seams, swells beehives until the honey trickles
down to oasis. You said, lift up the cup gently to your
lips and drink lest you spill. The warm sunlight seductively
filters through the baobab branches onto my hungry skin, oval slits
of light swaying with the wind that moves the palm-shaped leaves.

Is there a true word so terrible to face? That creates such
anguish? Only in its absence, the vagueness of an articulated
absence that churns ghosts, births easy theories of dualism, and
memory of a childhood that dreamt what it cannot now fulfill leaving
a solitary poet staring into the abyss with nothing in front or behind,
the sole saxophonist in the middle of Oxford Square playing long
after the mourners have left. It once was beautiful. Wearing your martyr's
cap, you sat too long defenseless, a lone aeolian harp battling a screaming

wind that has set upon itself the role of redeeming the world. Thames River will not mummify as winter is not here. City lights flicker industrialization onto the river's glass. Your face is distorted by the city's disco lights, two dark eyes peering into the display of orgy that dances before them.

Every day the world ends with our eyes glued on the next shipment of happiness. Nightmares of land mines, sequestered Palestinians, and Zulus who no longer believe in either the pointed tip of Shaka's assegai or in the poet's pen. Let it hurtle along at the pace of my mind, baobab fiend sprout a branch, trip a thought, middle of inferno, take a plunge into the fire next time of a mind through which the world

whistles tunes of its madness. Shoot a straight arrow into the sky, create wavy parallels, dance opposites in its wake, I see your face actualizing the possibility of life, the fact of death. The police records show your prints on a beer bottle, a witness who was watching the orgy of depression asked you to dance, "I have to leave, I am almost late, but thanks," he said. "Another time then?" she asked. "Maybe, but not here." She watched your

black coat that hid your back till it was swallowed by the dancing bodies, one slice of darkness and then you spilled onto Wordsworth Street.

Welcoming Mortality Home

(For my late mother, Nyambura)

As a child on my way home,
roughened more by play
than the weight of my books,
I ran that short distance from
the cornerstone paved road
to our gate afraid that the trees
bowing so close to the ground
would surely give way.

It's funny that on departure
with the security of home being
only a hurried cup of tea
and a slice of bread away,
the sound of our heavy gate closing
behind me was not as daunting as my
fear of not finding my way back,
doomed to forever roam in the distance
between yesterday and tomorrow
where familiarity and knowing become
a memory that neither fades nor grows.
But return or departure—I wanted to stay.

You once said that it was a long walk
to the beginning, starting with everything
just to lose all in the end. The end
of your life was the beginning of mine
you living long enough to walk me past
the enclaves of familiarity, past the bowing
trees hoping that on return I would be wise

enough to know that I too would lose all
in the end, that my lease on life would end.
If my end will be another's beginning,
if my hand will guide another just but
a few steps than you did me and that other
one step for another, will we not own
the sun? Will the end not always
be a better beginning?

My truth?
Once, when I could have stayed, I didn't.
Once, when I could have come back,
I called to say, I love you.

My Grandfather's Hands

My Grandfather's hands got tired before his feet,

his mind, and heart. Wars—assegai to bayonet,

Maxim to AK-47s, bodies of enemies and comrades

all shrouded and carried by his hands.

Independence—plantations picking tea by day

watching other people's homes, machete

in hand by night—his hands burying friends, lovers, and wives.

And on the evening of burying the last of everyone

—my grandmother—he looked at his hands and said

to us so young then, "When I am gone, bury me with your

hands." Then he smiled.

Letter to My Artist Friend Who Died Young

I find you sitting heavy between her and me, your death forcing
the split until our strained hands could no longer clasp—last
touches light as feathers—her, mourning your absence, me
celebrating the freedom of one who found the death
we imagined for ourselves. How else could I have kept you alive?
Looking back, I now know that you first practiced how to die

circling a bull's-eye around your heart, holding an empty gun
to your head, snapping a rope for tautness, lining crushed pills
like a million ants. Drowning certainly strikes me as a most
uninspired last photograph though opium and tuberculosis
were never any more dignified. What truths did you discover
that gave lie to a long life? That life never recovers from the pain

of birth? Our lives a series of darkened corners life always painted
black, always bleak like poverty and skin that life itself is a middle
passage? And me, am I to be pitied for finding life before death?
Your Grecian urn, to be frozen in last photographs, never to know
what it is to leave your best imprint. We were so brave and so young
that we could find music where there was none and dance to the hum

of silence. Elyria Projects in search of marijuana—it's morning
the sun easily coming through the old rainbow-color curtains
like raindrops through torn tin roofs. The sun bounces off beer
bottles, ricochets against needles and pipes. She is singing to let the day
in, giving escape to inhaled smoke. Quiet and the bottle of possibility
closes the world—darkens into permanent eclipse.

Your photograph finds her voice scratched and wounded a later
Lady Day who will not rise yet keeps falling. She never did say good-bye
yours having been enough. Just a letter that followed me from Elyria

town to the obscure town like fate. "There can be no space between life and death," she wrote on the photo that traced her voice. A last photograph through shredded clouds revealing bits of a blue sky

your reflection a shadow and you saying "art does not bleed, mother-fucking art does not bleed, shit, even vacuums contain the paradox of absence." For some suicide is first an implosion, but you, on your face you wore death like a fresh wound. Why was your camera found by the river, lens capped, a blind spectator to your death? Were it not an accident or a murder wouldn't your last photograph have been a portrait of your last breath?

Eight Months and Two Days
Loading Trucks at UPS

Siren running on metal. Rush through guard posts, Kaffir
in modern-day Appalachian coal mines, Jo'Burg diamond
mines. Live by dying a little each day. File and walk down
steps that echo dreams that once held a book, a promise
to the one who died haunted by chains that wouldn't break
and how he muttered "the first man to die for independence

was a black man" till the weight of his words crushed him.
It's Atlanta summer, even stones bleed, hell is a metal oven
box holding a loaf of bread. Bleed sweat till it furrows small
deposits of sweat, till muscles collapse into bone—the guillotine
is warmed by blood of many. We have pride, "A man must
sweat for a living, we are men doing men's work." But a break

is coming. A pop, an undercurrent of human pain, a hum under
hungry machines that rides under the wave of the worker's union.
A Goliath of a man wails, back snapped in two. The siren
again. It's break time. "Watch yourself, paycheck wrecks,"
a Haitian sings. I step into the sun, Gerald Double Shift
is holding his dreams, a worn-out ivory chess board, and I

settle for battle, cigarette in mouth. "You the only nigger I know
who smokes Camels," he keeps observing as he smokes
his Newport cigs. "Don't need no fiberglass in my diet," I always
reply. He moves, ten minutes from now between the heave
and shove of heavy packages, I will be thinking of moves
I could have made. Siren wails. As we walk back slow

like prisoners back to their cells, I sand my hand on jeans
to receive a photograph from Gerald's wallet, "That's my daughter.
She starts college in September." He stops and stares at his scarred
hands, "History has it that black is the building block, but why
the fucking bottom?" Siren wails. 5:30 p.m. Up the steps
guard posts, body search, and we pile into the train. A man

sits quietly in his derangement. Atlanta is strange, too many crazy
motherfuckers. We rack another game of chess, and I think how
as a child I always played black. It's payday, we will end up
in a bar, shoot a little pool, talk about life. If Big Johnny hadn't
snapped his back, he would have showed up high.

Logotherapy

My son was only nine years old when he died
two years ago. Now, I cannot hold anything
not even a pail of water for washing without
remembering his embrace. I call out his name
"Elias, Elias! What story shall I read you tonight?"
Everything even my pen and paper I have named
after him. Jealous Death came for me last night
an old man and we walked to the Grand Canyon.
There he showed me what would be mine
the peace of naming things by their names
of my Elias not dying every time I hold something
in my arms. He said, "All you have to do is stop
renaming the world after your son. God does not like it."
For peace, I was tempted but for love, I told him
he was crazy to think I can forget my Elias. He walked
me from my sleep to the morning with a promissory
note worth two days. In my hand now
I have two days to name God Elias.

To My Archeologist

When you find my bones, do not be any gentler than my life
was—that whispery fracture across my ulna—a tumble
and a fall—six years old. And that fissure in the tubular with sand
and soil running along it like ants—a civil war in the streets
of Nairobi. There are things of myself that you will not find
things that would not keep well with me in the ground.
Ordinary things. Of what use would it be to bury me
with roast goat meat, cheesecakes, and my Lagavulin scotch?
And why would I want to live on in death without them?
I have to reconsider your offer. You will not have my bones.
Instead of an afterlife in a stranger's museum, I choose fire.
Let my ashes rain through your sift. I want to be gone.
And when all those that remember me are gone
I will finally be done and over with this life.

V

Gifts of Violence

Gifts of Violence

A caught Tilapia fish in my hands
fighting for breath

Shaken but hungry I unhook
throw it back mid-stroke

with a word to heal, soothe
the wound of spiked feed.

Moon comes with night
to illuminate my palms

now glistening with soft
scales hard like words.

Faith

Standing in the middle of the earth
when it splits in two. All around there
is nothing—below, hell as I imagined it.
Trees skeletons, it's cold, clouds bleed
their acid and tomorrow so alien
like death. Yesterday, peace came
in many forms, you speaking for me
oil and canvas, earth, clay. I drop
my sorrow in any given ocean
and God can no longer mirror himself.

JailBirds

As Hurricane Sandy gathers wind and steam,

I slowly drive down I-84 East trying to make

it home before I get walled in by hard sheets of rain.

My headlights catch a ball of yellow, brown, and golden

edged leaves falling like a waterfall down a tree falling

to the earth, and somewhere between the branch and the ground

blue jay birds break out of the nest and for a second

they dip toward the fast-coming ground, then fly away

leaving behind them an angry explosion of leaves.

And what had been their home or prison, a tall tree, broken

by Sandy now on bended knee holding onto to its kin.

Fall

Fall is here. As a gentle ghost
hisses past the maple tree
a last single purple red
leaf, ripe by what it must become
loses grip—a faltering dance—such grace
to its grave where hungry roots await
to be fed spring. It's death with a promise
of resurrection. To catch fish, the bait
is best rotten.

To the Driver Who Splashed
Me with Rainwater

Whether a pedestrian on the sidewalk,
commuter in the train, or driver in a car
we all keep pace with our own death,
so thanks for the cold blessing, but all
the same may you find yours sooner.

Dread Locks

Dread-locked I was locked
in a game of truth or dare.
Truth.
Do you take drugs?
No.
Laughter.
Truth or dare the cops will lock
me up anyway.

Revolt

I

Inside Berlin Conference,
they keep tearing
into black skin, naming
each tear for themselves

II

Heart keeps beating, alone,
with them, in them, outside
of them, a grenade resting
in their uneven gardens

III

Now, every so often, a nigger
black as night palms master's
flashlight to find truth of red
blood. *Fuck* negritude!

IV

Who will protect you from the storm
we are gathering?

Prints of Genocide

Ashes from mass cremations
filter into our suburbia parks.
"My dear, no it's not gold dust.
Do not play outside until it passes.
Black rain then white clouds."

I Swear I See Skulls Coming

It's strange artwork, perhaps voodoo,
a human skull strung in perfect symmetry
to a tree in Mount Kenya forest,
it's grinning away a sole bullet hole

now jagged. It certainly adds a twist
to the aeolian harp, doesn't it? Art
is inspired in many ways,
here it's death whistling in the wind.

Probe. Measurements not racist but
racialist. Could have been a white
tourist or a black native. It must
have held a sizable brain. Not mind—

philosophy is not in bone or DNA. Let's
call it a colonial relic. Facts, known
to unknown. Rwanda manufactures 400,000
skulls a year. See the movement

here? Death-art-Science-social history-
a perfect dialectic. Nairobi National
Archives, a modern building with feet
sinking in slum, "Skull of a colonial relic

on display." It's clean. "I swear that thing
whistles at night, winds in a middle passage,"
the curator says. Here I must come clean.
The poet cannot speak of the unknown,

but I walk outside to see a whole country
walking with guns held to their heads.

Kenya

Inside looking out, snow is falling and I am thinking
how happy we once were, when promises and dreams
came easy and how when we, lovers covered only

by a warm Eldoret night, you waved a prophecy
at a shooting star and said, "When the time comes
we shall name our first child Kenya," and how I

laughed and said, "Yes, our child then shall be country
and human" and we held hands, rough and toughened
by shelling castor seeds. My dear, when did our

clasped hands become heavy chains and anchors holding
us to the mines and diamond and oil fields? Our hands
calloused by love and play, these same hands—when

did they learn to grip a machete or a gun to spit hate?
And this earth that drinks our blood like a hungry child
this earth that we have scorched to cinders—when we

are done eating it, how much of it will be left for Kenya?
My dear, our child is born, is dying. Tomorrow the child
will be dead.

This Is What I Know

*(*For LGBT Africans)*

I know that Black people were sold as slaves because they were seen as talking beasts of burden and Africans colonized for their own good; and it was unnatural for women to operate heavy machinery let alone operate on a brain.

I know that in the United States, Jim Crow used the rope to keep black from white, and apartheid in South Africa killed for as little as looking across the color line; and that intermarrying between the races was a crime against God, Queen, and Country.

I know that a God of many names, the laws of many lands, science and nature were used to justify slavery and colonialism, holocausts and genocides, rapes and lynching.

I know that African dictators called those who fought for democracy "puppets under the pay of foreign masters" and the foreign masters called those same people communists and insurgents.

And this I know very well: that had the Sojourner Truths, Dedan Kimathis, Martin Luther Kings, Malcom Xs, and Ruth Firsts failed, my wife and I would not have crossed the color line and my daughter would not have been possible.

I know that she, just like her mother and me, just like her grandparents, will have her struggles, but it will BE a struggle waged at the crossroad of many cultures and worlds.

So I must know that those before me did not die so that I could use my freedom to put others in jail; or use the same laws that betrayed them to enslave and torture.

I must know that if Steve Biko died so I could write what I like, then my pen cannot become the weapon that justifies the torture and murder of others.

How then can I not know that no one appointed me protector of African cultural purity? How can I not know that I am not the standard of all that is moral and natural?

What fortress is this I build that subjugates those within and keeps those outside under siege? Whose moral law is this I use to judge?

Whose legal system to jail? Whose weapon to murder? And whose tongue do I use to silence?

How can I, Black and African and blessed as I am by the struggles of my fathers and mothers deny my gay brothers and sisters their rights?

Epilogue

(For Ron Wallace)

Having broken through the picket line

into the State Street Barnes and Noble

in this time of war

I am leafing through *Long for This World*

until I am stopped

by "why I am not a nudist"

—a poem about sending the seen

back into the unseen

or returning the nude

into the folds of the mind.

Here, words

are like black-

and-white passport

photographs

that cover patches

of her flesh until the poet

can recollect

all of her in the moment

between waking up and getting up.

Lightning Source UK Ltd.
Milton Keynes UK
UKHW010629090421
381705UK00001B/23